The Barnyard Bunch

CLUCKY CHICKENS

Ryan James

NORWOOD HOUSE PRESS

Cataloging-in-Publication Data

Names: James, Ryan.
Title: Clucky chickens / Ryan James.
Description: Buffalo, NY : Norwood House Press, 2026. | Series: The barnyard bunch | Includes glossary and index.
Identifiers: ISBN 9781978574236 (pbk.) | ISBN 9781978574243 (library bound) | ISBN 9781978574250 (ebook)
Subjects: LCSH: Chickens--Juvenile literature. | Livestock--Juvenile literature.
Classification: LCC SF487.5 J359 2026 | DDC 636.5--dc23

Published in 2026 by
Norwood House Press
2544 Clinton Street
Buffalo, NY 14224

Designer: Rhea Magaro
Editor: Kim Thompson

Photo credits: Cover, p.1 Cj Nattanai/Shutterstock.com; p. 5 Wirestock Creators/Shutterstock.com; p. 6 pets in frames/Shutterstock.com; p. 7 ang intaravichian/Shutterstock.com; p. 8Pressmaster/Shutterstock.com; p. 9 Julia Lopatina/Shutterstock.com; p. 10 Gagarin Iurii/Shutterstock.com; p. 11 Alekcey/Shutterstock.com; pp. 12, 13 Robert Adamec/Shutterstock.com; p. 14 Coryn/Shutterstock.com; p. 15 sergey kolesnikov/Shutterstock.com; p. 17 IRA_EVVA/Shutterstock.com; p. 18 Alterego/Shutterstock.com; p. 19andia/Shutterstock.com; p. 21 Nick Beer/Shutterstock.com;

Printed in the United States of America

CPSIA compliance information: Batch #CSNHP26: For further information contact Norwood House Press at 1-800-237-9932.

TABLE OF CONTENTS

CLUCKY CHICKENS

Chickens are farm animals. They live in the barnyard.

HOW CHICKENS LOOK

Chickens are birds. They are covered in **feathers**. Their feathers come in many different colors.

Chickens have two legs. They have short **beaks**.

Chickens have **wattles** on their chins.

They have **combs** on their heads.

HOW CHICKENS SOUND

Chickens cluck to **communicate**. They squawk if **predators** are near.

Chickens growl to give a warning.

This tells enemies to stay away.

Roosters are male chickens.

They crow at **dawn**. It sounds like "cock-a-doodle-doo."

WHAT CHICKENS EAT

Chickens are **omnivores**. They eat many different foods.

Farmers feed seeds and **grains** to chickens.

Chickens will also eat fruits and vegetables. They even eat insects and slugs!

HOW CHICKENS GROW UP

Hens are female chickens. They lay eggs. They sit on the nest to keep the eggs warm.

In about 21 days, baby chickens **hatch**. They are called chicks.

FUN ON THE FARM

Chickens like to play. They try to reach high places. This gives them a good view of what is happening all over the farm.

GLOSSARY

beaks (beeks): the hard, pointed parts on the mouths of chickens

combs (kohmz): the soft red parts on the tops of chickens' heads

communicate (kuh-MYOO-ni-kate): to share information and feelings

dawn (dawn): the beginning of the day when the sun rises

feathers (FETH-urz): the light, soft parts that cover a chicken's body and keep it warm

grains (graynz): cereal plants such as wheat, corn, and oats

hatch (hach): to break out of an egg to be born

omnivores (AHM-nuh-vorz): animals that eat both plants and meat

predators (PRED-uh-turz): wolves and other animals that hunt chickens for food

wattles (WAH-tuhlz): the soft red parts found under a chicken's chin

THINKING QUESTIONS

1. Name three body parts that chickens have.
2. How long does it take for a chick to hatch from an egg?
3. What do chickens eat?
4. How do chickens communicate?
5. What are male and female chickens called?

INDEX

ABOUT THE AUTHOR

Ryan James lives in the mountains of North Carolina, where he goes hiking with his dog Bailey. He loves fly fishing, visiting farms in the area, and picking fresh produce. He has always enjoyed writing and wrote his first book as a teenager.